INDIA'S INTELLECTUAL DESERT

D1871295

INDIA'S INTELLECTUAL DESERT

V.T. Rajshekar

GYAN

© **Author**

All rights reserved. No part of this book may be reproduced, stored, adapted, or transmitted in any form or by any means, electronic, mechanical, photocopying, micro-filming, recording or otherwise, or translated in any language, without the prior written permission of the copyright owner and the publisher. The book is sold subject to the condition that it shall not, by way of trade or otherwise, be lent, resold, hired out, or otherwise circulated without the prior publisher's written consent in any form of binding or cover other than that in which it is published.

The views and opinions expressed in this book are author(s) own and the facts reported by them have been verified to the extent possible, and the publishers are not in any way liable for the same.

ISBN : 978-81-212-1290-8

First Published, 2015

Published by

Gyan Publishing House
23, Main Ansari Road, Darya Ganj,
New Delhi- 110 002
Ph. : 2328 2060, 2326 1060
E-mail: books@gyanbooks.com

Printed at : Reliable Infomedia, New Delhi

Cataloging in Publication Data—DK
Courtesy: D.K. Agencies (P) Ltd. <docinfo@dkagencies.com>

Rajshekar Shetty, V. T., 1932- **author.**
India's intellectual desert / V.T. Rajshekar.
pages cm
Reprint.
ISBN 9788121212908

1. Intellectuals—India. 2. India—Intellectual life. I. Title.

DDC 305.5520954 23

INTRODUCTION

The essay may be devastating. But true. True from our point of view.

Truth is always bitter, unpleasant, hurting. But it has to be told. Did they not tell us: *Satya Meva Jayate* (truth shall triumph)? "Know the Truth, and Truth shall make you free", said the Bible (John 8:32).

In this we have tried to speak out the Truth to the best of our ability and provoke the thinking sections. Then only the society can start thinking and try to save itself. As Untouchables forming the base of the country's social pyramid, our view is always from the bottom of the society.

This view from the bottom may be ugly but we can't help it. Because we did not create this ugly society.

The mind manipulators have conditioned us in such a way making us think that "money corruption" is the only form of corruption sapping our vitals. The media is full of corruption stories. Books that have come out on corruption are best-sellers. People are arrested daily and tried on corruption charges. But no top corrupt person has been so far convicted. Kings of corruption are roaming round and delivering lectures on ethics. Stories on corruption have become music to our ears. Those "fighting corruption" have become instant heroes.

But the poverty of our thinking is so much that we don't realise the simple thing that as long as there is a bribe-giver there is a bribe-taker. This entire exercise— wasting so much of time, energy and money — on corruption is a waste because the bribe-giver and the bribe-taker belong to the same class.

The mind manipulators have succeeded in diverting our attention to a non-issue and making the society obsessed with corruption. And yet corruption is increasing by leaps and bounds because we are a corrupt society.

There is a method in this madness. This crazy "drive against corruption" is to hide the more serious forms of corruption.

There are four varieties of corruption:(1) Money corruption. (2) Moral corruption. (3) Caste corruption. (4) Intellectual corruption.

The "corruption cases" that normally make front-page headlines are those involving only money corruption. The mind-manipulators are highlighting only one form of corruption to deliberately hide the other three forms of corruption — particularly the last one.

Of the four, the "intellectual corruption" is the king of all corruptions.

If the "intellecual class" of India had been free from corruption we would have succeeded by this time to control all the other three forms of corruption, particularly the money corruption with which we are so much obsessed.

India's intellectual class has become so corrupt that it is deliberately diverting the society's attention to money corruption which is a small part of the overall world of corruption. This book tries to explore this intellectual corruption with a ringside seat inside this cloistered convent.

A section of this intellectual class may say that we have made a sweeping indictment. No. We are fully aware that every rule has an exception. In fact, the exceptions do prove the rule. Such glorious exceptions to the rule — the unsung heroes of the intellectual class — have at least saved our society from death and destruction. This is an attempt to make the silent angry and speak out. And also impress such of them that there is nothing like a "silent intellectual".

The frauds are ruling because of the silence of such honest intellectuals.

New Delhi **V.T. Rajshekar**

October 1, 1999

The sudden fall of President Suharto, heading one of the giant Asian Tigers, Indonesia, in the year 1998 following a powerful student uprising coupled with a country-wide unrest and the quick exit of his "crony caucus" one by one, made us think why India's stinkingly corrupt rulers, who made a total mess of the country, have not only been never punished but allowed to rule despite pushing India to the wall and making it the world's largest beggar country.

What may be the cause of India's gradual decay, fall and slow death? Despite 50 years of "independence" maturity, why are we still acting like imbeciles, impotent, downright stupid despite having the world's second largest population and a glorious historical past?

Definition of intellectual: Dr. Babasaheb Ambedkar, the Father of India and the 20th century India's tallest intellectual titan, has diagnosed the disease affecting India. And his prophetic words need repetition:

> Whether you accept the theory of the great man as the maker of history or whether you do not, this much you will have to concede that in every country the intellectual class is the most influential class, if not the governing class. The intellectual class is the class which can foresee, it is the class which can advise and give lead. In no country does the mass of the people live the life of intelligent thought and action. It is largely imitative and follows the intellectual class. There is no exaggeration in saying that the entire destiny of a country depends upon its intellectual class. If the intellectual class is honest, independent and disinterested it can be trusted to take the initiative and give a proper lead when a crisis arises. It is true that intellect by itself is no virtue. It is only a means and the use of means depends upon the ends which an intellectual person pursues. An intellectual man can be a good man but he can easily be a rogue. Similarly an intellectual class may be a band of high-souled persons, ready to help, ready to emancipate erring humanity or it may easily be a gang of crooks or a body of advocates of a narrow clique from which it draws its support.

> You may think it a pity that the intellectual class in India is simply another name for the Brahmin caste. You may regret that the two are one; that the existence of the intellectual class should be bound with one single caste, that this intellectual class should share the interest and the aspirations of that Brahmin caste, which has regarded itself the custodian of the interest of that caste, rather than of the interests of the country. All this may be very regrettable. But the fact remains that the Brahmins form the intellectual class of the Hindus. It is not only an intellectual class but it is a class which is held in great reverence by the rest of the Hindus. The Hindus are taught that the Brahmins are *Bhudevatas* (Gods on earth). The Hindus are taught that Brahmins alone can be their teachers. Manu says, "If it be asked how it should be with respect to points of the Dharma which have not been specially mentioned, the answer is that which Brahmins who are Shishthas propound shall doubtless have legal force".
>
> (*Dr. Babasaheb Ambedkar Writings & Speeches* Vol.I, p. 71, Maharashtra Govt. Publication, 1979)

Was Dr. Ambedkar wrong?

India's rulers who hold the Untouchables in contempt may dismiss Babasaheb's verdict with derision because he was an Untouchable. A Hindu believes what he wants to believe. But here we are concerned with that very Hindu belief system that has not only made topsy-turvy of the country's entire socio-economic-political system but brought the very thinking to a standstill.

Deaf & dumb class: During our 25-years as a journalist in the *Indian Express* in different parts of India and later as the Editor of *Dalit Voice* for the past about 20 years, many times we had come to some tentative conclusions. But now our views are getting crystalized and we are presenting them in this essay though we are pretty sure the rulers of India will once again dismiss it with contempt.

We are not worried about what the ruling class will say about us. Our worry is about our deaf and dumb "intellectual class" which has never played the role of a disturber of the status quo.

During the latest Indonesian crisis, the intellectual class of that country shouted in unison and asked Suharto and his cronies to get out. And their voice was heard and listened to with respect. Suharto and his cronies were the rulers and they brought affluence to Indonesia and made it a powerful Asian Tiger. The intellectual class too was benefited from the ruling class affluence. Yet this class had the courage of conviction to protest and pull down Suharto.

Do we have such a class of intellectuals in India? The Indian intellectuals are a class by themselves. They always worship the rising sun, their public posture can be always predicted and easily persuaded into some slogan. During the Emergency (1977), Prime Minister Indira Gandhi merely asked these intellectuals to bend but they literally crawled.

These intellectuals are an incorrigible class. Neither it has learnt anything new nor it has forgotten anything old. The only art it has mastered is never, ever to give publicity to any dissenter. Those who question the status-quo should be mercilessly suppressed by any means.

Suppression through silence: This writer was one such victim of this intellectual class. Despite about 20 years of publishing our journal, *Dalit Voice* , and numerous other books to our credit, this intellectual class was deliberately silent on our work. Suppression through silence is the deadliest weapon of this intellectual class and we have been its cruelest victims.

This intellectual class knows the danger of giving publicity to any work that challenges the rulers. Because they know it is fire. And fire will burn and burn them first. Hence this suppression through silence.

Its silence on our work both in the *Dalit Voice,* the oldest and the largest circulated intellectual journal of the "*Persecuted Nationalities Denied Human Rights*", and a series of books published by our Dalit Sahitya Akademy is exactly on these lines. Its silence on every case of widespread, grave injustice and crime perpetrated on the over 85% of the country's oppressed people — particularly the Untouchables, Tribals and women — is unparalleled in the intellectual part of this world. The outside world hardly knows anything about these crimes which are covered in the gandhian garb of non-violence.

India's "national" papers: The ruling class of every country hides its crimes. We know that. The American White rulers are silent on their racist crimes against 20% of its own Black (African-American) nationals. Yet the American White intellectual class has produced Naom Chomsky and many more. The British, German, French and all other countries have their protesters, deserters, detractors and that is how the White Western people, despite all their shortcomings, are dominating the world with their contribution. The credit for this goes only to its brave intellectual class. The Western intellectuals have the courage to question their respective country's rulers. That is why they have become great.

But, alas, what we have in India is not creative drivers but intimidating head-hunters like our yellow journalist Arun Shourie who wrote a puffy book maligning India's tallest intellectual titan, Dr. Babasaheb Ambedkar, on behalf of the ruling class, won name and fame, awards and rewards, bagfull of money and finally a seat in Parliament.

India's only intellectual journal: Since journalists gate-crash into this world of intellectuals (**exceptions to this rule need not get annoyed because exceptions do prove the rule)**, we need to mention this class of yellow brigade, India's "national" toilet papers. The only "intellectual" journal this yellow brigade is able to raise and sustain is the *Economic and Political Weekly* (EPW).

Carrying a copy of EPW till recently was considered a sign of intellectualism in India. But if you hear the circulation figure of this journal it is shocking. Poor EPW is confined to library rooms and hardly read. We had a meeting with the Editor of this journal in Bombay over a decade back and requested him to reduce its "leftist fervour" cultivated by a section of India's intellectuals. It used to be fashionable to call oneself a marxist and flaunt a copy of the EPW. Even those days are over. Marxism in India is the other name for brahminism. And even in the two states where the marxists are running the government the rulers continue to belong to the same class/caste. In other words, the EPW is not considered an anti-establishment, anti-status quo, or anti-ruling class journal. The journal gets ads from all rich and powerful business houses — a privilege never conferred upon the *Dalit Voice*.

The rag-tag world of Indian journalism comprises tired, sick columnists who spin out their gutter journalism to entertain the reading public. These journalists do not enlighten the readers. As bum-lickers of the ruling class, they enjoy good life and hence move heaven and earth to maintain the status quo. No original thinking, no refreshing thought. They dare not speak out the truth. Rather, they amend the truth.

Investigative journalism: Each journalist has become the tail of some political leader or political party and his secret of survival is not the popularity of his column and its appeal to public conscience but the publicity he derives out of the publication of his yellow garbage. Racketeers in TV and print media parading as journalists are hand-in-glove with the rulers and the publicity they get keep them alive. It is an all-round conspiracy in India to undercut the truth and continue the exploitative game.

Recently, there was much uproar in the press about the Press Council chief, Justice P.B. Sawant's criticism of the *Times of*

India using its columns to defend its owner's misdeeds. The entire lot of journalists and even editors joined this chorus of attack on poor Justice Sawant who stood his ground. Editor H.K. Dua came out with some half- truths only when he was sacked for not supporting the *Times of India* tycoon's misdeeds.

Charge against *Times of India*. The mischief in the media was further exposed by Ajit Bhattacharjea but he had hardly any supporters:-

> A week has passed, at the time of writing, since the Press Council of India announced that it had censured *The Times of India* in the strongest terms for trying to misuse the services of an Editor for the personal benefit of the proprieter of the paper. It praised the journalist concerned, Mr. H.K. Dua, for resisting the pressure though the refusal cost him his job. He had complained to the Press Council.
>
> For such a charge to be levelled against the oldest English language daily in the country, and one that claims the highest circulation, undeniably makes news. The journalist victimised was well-known in the profession: he had served as Editor-in-Chief of *The Hindustan Times* and *The Indian Express* before joining *The Times of India*. And the issues raised in the detailed 69-page judgment of the Council concern the independence of the Editor and the credibility of the Press, matters of considerable public interest.
>
> Yet, not a single major English language newspaper with head-quarters in Delhi has printed a line of the Press Council's verdict, though it was sent to them and the news agencies distributed a summary. It was ignored by *The Times of India*, though papers censured by the Press Council are expected to publish findings against them to guard against repetition of such offences. Of the English-language papers I have seen, only *The Hindu* of Chennai, *Deccan Herald* of Bangalore, *Deccan Chronicle* of Hyderabad and *Tribune* of Chandigarh published a summary.
>
> Such self-censorship by the major national newspapers published in the Capital is more disturbing than the misdemeanour of an individual paper. If the Press is to perform

the role expected of it in a democracy, society has the right to know whether editors are subject to pressures that could affect the credibility of the paper. Blacking out the issue could suggest that the newspapers may be interested in keeping such delicate matters away from the public gaze.

Some editors may feel that the Press Council's verdict is unfair or too sweeping. Such views have been expressed before. If so, a paper is free to point out flaws. But not to publish such a serious charge against a leading paper by a body created by Parliament to oversee the conduct of the Press is indefensible. Self-censorship hurts the credibility of the Press more grievously than externally-imposed censorship.

Credibility is the oxygen of the Press. It can be maintained only if newspapers are seen to be as anxious to expose those among them guilty of misusing their powers as they are to expose misuse of political and bureaucratic authority.

(*Hindu,* Feb.17, 1999).

Journalists give free advice to others, particularly politicians. But they follow none. The higher you go in the hierarchy, the corruption is too much. And intellectual corruption is the worst form of corruption. And that is why the influence of intellectuals in India is minimal if not non-existent. In the US, the President consults the academicians and top journalists. But in India, no one bothers about our intellectuals because they have turned careerists.

Defective reporting: Justice P.B. Sawant, chairman of the Press Council of India, came under attack because he spoke out the truth on the corruption in the Indian press:

Jaipur: The chairman of the Press Council of India, Mr. Justice P.B. Sawant, has expressed that newspapers also could be brought under the purview of the Consumer Protection Act. Perhaps the reader should be given the right as consumer to seek redressal in the case of inaccurate/inadequate/ defamatory reporting.

It is yet to be seen whether incorrect/incomplete reporting can

> be termed defective reporting. It is a moot question how a decision can be reached. Yet it is worth trying.
>
> Justice Sawant said that the freedom of the press, ensured as a fundamental right in the Constitution, was not the freedom of the publisher/printer/Editor or even the reporter. "It is the freedom of the people to be informed adequately and accurately". The press has become an institution wielding enormous powers. "It can make and unmake governments. It can cause civil deaths to persons and institutions. Yet there is no regulatory mechanism for the media in this country", he lamented.
>
> (*Hindu* Feb.15, 1999).

The suggestion made by Justice Sawant needs serious consideration because this press has become a law unto itself. The people have to intervene so that their sovereignty is not impinged.

Collective conspiracy: Says Harish Khare in whose writings we have always found some sparks of brilliance and original thinking:

> That brings us to the role of journalists. It is by default that they have come to be treated as intellectuals. An overwhelming number of newsmen employed in the print media are unequipped to undertake any intellectual enterprise and they are not even apologetic about it. It is only a tiny minority that seems to have succeeded in usurping the role of the intelligentsia, largely because they have access to an effective forum that contrasts sharply with the timorousness of the state-run TV and radio.
>
> (*Times of India*, Jan.21, 1988. Harish Khare is now with the *Hindu* in Delhi).

The much publicised "investigative journalism" died soon after ousting A.R. Antulay as Chief Minister of Maharashtra just because he was a Muslim. No daily or periodical speaks about "investigative journalism" today because each media institution is run by a big business house which fears if "investigative journalism" is encouraged, a rival media will start "investigating" its corruption and the stink in its backyard. So, as a part of this collective conspiracy India's national "toilet" papers have bid a good-bye to investigative journalism. Because everybody is a thief.

We can understand the rulers indulging in exploiting the weak. Rulers became rulers only by exploiting the weak. But the tragedy gets awesome when intellectuals become highway robbers and join this collective piracy.

Hypocrisy on English: Because of this intellectual skull-duggery, hardly any intellectual discussion takes place either in the media or on public platform. The main reason for this lack of intellectual atmosphere is that the English literacy is confined to less than 2% of India's population and in India a person is considered intellectual only if he can write in English. That sums up the intellectual poverty of India.

About 50% of India's population is totally illiterate and the Indian language literacy is also small. But more than that, this class is divided because of language barriers. The English literate class claiming to be intellectual is a microscopic minority and this minority wants to maintain its monopoly over its status by denying literacy to the rest. The English language, the symbol of status and prestige, is deliberately denied to the masses. Only English dailies are called "national" newspapers but learning English is dubbed "anti-national." How do you like it? But India's English-educated intellectuals are silent on this hypocrisy as the ruling class has put a bar on English education. Such is the depth of dishonesty of our intellectuals.

Philosopher-king: Such an appalling situation is unparalleled in the world and India also gets the credit for keeping its 1,000 million population poverty-stricken and hence forced to remain destitute. Can we think of a greater crime than this committed by India's intellectual class?

Intellectuals are a rare breed. They have to uphold truth, suffer for truth and justice. And will not hesitate to die in pursuit of truth and justice.

Julien Benda (*Treason of the Intellectuals*, London, Norton, 1980) defined intellectuals as a tiny band of super-gifted and endowed philosopher-kings who constitute the conscience of mankind.

When erosion of moral values of a society takes serious proportions, the honest intellectual's honest conscience gets disturbed forcing him to intervene and rescue the society. We find only one soul in India coming nearest to this profile of our intellectuals. And that is Dr. Babasaheb B.R. Ambedkar. He became the scourge and scavenger of the society not afraid of attacking and exposing even the "Father of the Nation", even when M.K. Gandhi was alive. That is the courage of his conviction.

In defence of Brahmin woman: As an intellectual, we cannot find a better example in the whole country than Babasaheb. He was a source of inspiring ideas and was ready to sacrifice and suffer to bring about social change and social justice among the suffering millions of this land. He was the one and only intellectual of the country who felt for the suffering of even Hindus, and recommended the destruction of their caste system (*Chaturvarna*)— and particularly the Brahmin women. He introduced the Hindu Code Bill as India's first Law Minister and later resigned when Brahmins and other upper castes led by Pandit Nehru opposed this Bill. Though he was a bitter critic of Hindus and their Hinduism, he suffered for Hindus and resigned as a Union Minister for their sake.

His whole life was devoted to bring about social justice which is being denied to not only Dalits and all other oppressed "low castes" but even to Brahmin women. We can't find a single parallel in the whole of "independent" India who suffered, sacrificed and finally died for the sake of liberating the country and its oppressed millions. Babasaheb, therefore, is the one and the only model we have before us and it is keeping him as our ideal, we have written this essay.

An honest intellectual is one whose spirit cannot be extinguished by threats. Nor torture alter his conviction. His goals are clear and he is prepared to sacrifice, suffer and die to achieve his goals. For him, suffering itself turns into joy.

Role of social scientists: Upper castes have also produced any number of intellectuals but they don't fit into this definition because when their caste interests come into clash with reality, they shirk and slip into silence. The common reply of such an intellectual in times of crisis is: "Why should we enter into this controversy?" They just throw up their hands and withdraw. An honest intellectual cannot afford to be neutral or silent.

During the anti-Mandal Commission agitation many such intellectuals got exposed. The Mandal Commission stood for social justice for the Backward Castes who constitute a staggering 55% of the country's population. Social justice is the foundation on which the country's Constitution is built but noted social scientists like M.N. Srinivas, Andre Betellie, Roy-Burman etc. did not behave like social scientists but advocates of their *jati* cause. (*Dalit Voice*, April 16, 1994 p.8-11: "*M.N. Srinivas & His brahminical values*", Dr. C. Parvathamma). This is the problem with all Indian social scientists who also belong to the upper castes. When their caste interests come into clash with social justice, they either sulk, sit silent or become campaign managers for their caste. This is the main reason why in India social scientists are not taken seriously. The government rarely consults them. The industry never bothers about them though in a country devoid of social justice, social scientists should have been the most sought after experts.

Hindu war on Sikhs: When the ruling class of India declared a war on Sikhs for demanding self-determination, these intellectuals also turned out to be Hindus and prostituted their press. *Dalit Voice* fought for justice and truth and also suffered and sacrificed. We were arrested under the Terrorist Act and jailed. The Editor of the *Tribune*, a leading English daily published from Chandigarh, was earlier our Resident Editor at the *Indian Express*, Bangalore. Being a Brahmin, his sympathies went with his *jatwalas* and his writings then were full of criticism of "Sikh terrorists". This is what happens when intellectuals become blind because of their caste interests. Kuldip Nayar, though an upper caste Punjabi Hindu, stood by the Sikhs and proved to be an exception to this rule.

The point is, in India an intellectual cannot but be a prostitute. The system makes him a prostitute. This highly stratified Hindu society arranged on an ascending order of reverence and descending degree of contempt is a fertile breeding ground for such prostitutes. And that is how India has become a huge intellectual Sahara desert with not a single Indian getting the Nobel Prize after the "independence" (1947).

Nobel Prize for Amartya Sen: The only one who got the Nobel Prize, Amartya Sen, is not an Indian citizen and achieved all his name and fame after living in the West. But the Indian intellectual class went gaga over Amartya Sen and carried him over their heads and paraded him all over even as he rebuked them for ignoring the social justice aspect. But even Amartya Sen cannot be credited with 100% intellectual honesty. The burden of his song during his parade round India was that India's ruling class was denying primary education to the masses and social justice in its quest for economic prosperity. If he had been an honest intellectual, he should have known the truth. The truth is that if the rulers of India had assured social justice and implemented the constitutional directive of free, compulsory and universal primary education, the upper castes of India would have lost their rulership. Amartya Sen knew this truth and yet he was hiding the truth to remain popular with the rulers of India. Nay. Amartya himself belonged to a Bengali upper caste.

An honest intellectual, said Dr. Babasaheb Ambedkar, should be the scourge and scavenger of the society driven by metaphysical passion and disinterested principle of justice and truth. He/she is a merciless surgeon wielding the surgeon's knives mercilessly against all that is evil, denouncing corruption, defending the weak, exposing the humbug.

Did our Indian intellectuals ever act as the scourge and scavenger of the society? We have no instance of any such intellectual after Babasaheb. If there are any, we are not aware of such rare souls.

Even Amartya Sen enjoying the upper caste hospitality and the mad media buildup forgot what the great poet had said:

> "Where Truth is not suppressed, where history is not falsified and where frightened scholars do not shudder away from challenging details of access to documents... into that heaven of freedom, my father, let my country awake".

Is there any intellectual in India who meets this standard? If there is any, we are not aware of such a soul.

Suffering, sacrificing & dying: Julien Benda in his book identifies intellectuals as those "who denounce corruption, defend the weak, defy imperfect or oppressive authority". Real intellectuals, he says, must face the risk of being burnt alive, ostracised, or crucified. Such people will be naturally very small in number. Ordinary people can't take such heavy personal risks. And such powerful personalities will be very small in number. But every country, every society has at best a couple of such powerful personalities whose voice can choke a government. Is there any such personality in today's India?

During the Babri Masjid demolition, did those claiming to be authorities on Ancient Indian History like Romila Thapar and Sarvepalli Gopal, do anything visible to make this fact known? Did they protest, suffer and sacrifice? They might have issued some statements and delivered some speeches.

This writer had an occasion to confront S. Gopal at a seminar in Bangalore on this very issue. Obviously becoming irritated, he asked: "What more can you expect from me? You thought I should have committed suicide?"

Babri Masjid was a cause worth suffering, sacrificing and dying. That would have averted the death of thousands of innocent Muslims later. Babri Masjid was the greatest tragedy that the ruling class of India forced upon innocent Muslims after the "Blue Star Operation" that was launched to ensure *hinduisation* of Sikhs.

Falsification of history: S. Gopal, son of Sir Radhakrishnan, a former President of India, and an authority on Ancient Indian History and more than that a Brahmin, should have at least threatened self-immolation. Such a threat on the Babri Masjid issue would have sent shock waves all over the country and halted the Hindu nazi bid to demolish the Babri Masjid. Not to speak of actual self-immolation, this historian failed even to make a threat despite knowing the whole truth of Babri Masjid and having written a book of the same title. Alas, Indian "historians" allowed falsification of history because both falsifiers of history and these historians belonged to the same caste. In no other country, the historians would have allowed a noted historical monument to be grabbed by fascists calling it the birth place of a god. Indian historians failed and the country suffered a major war and violence. All because of the silence of our intellectuals.

But the same intellectuals of India pushed an unsuspecting youth to commit a fake self-immolation in Delhi (1990) when their caste interests were threatened by the implementation of the Mandal Commission report on Backward Castes.

So, from Benda's celebrated definition of intellectuals, can we declare Sarvepalli Gopal, an eminent historian on Ancient India, an intellectual? Can we call Romila Thapar an intellectual?

Both S. Gopal and Romila Thapar failed to speak out and much less act as the scourge and scavenger of the society during the Babri Masjid episode. Had the two teamed together and threatened self-immolation, the Hindu zealots and the government would have been forced to think and act. But these "historians" played safe and allowed the Hindu nazis to run riot because to them their *jati* interests became more important than the interests of the society and the country.

Historians perverting history: We repeat: an intellectual if he has to remain honest must be able to suffer, sacrifice and even die for the cause he or she holds dear. Both Romila Thapar and S. Gopal know the facts of history which say that Babri Masjid is a Muslim monument but they surrendered and allowed themselves to be silenced. They failed to speak out the truth for the sake of private gains. Had they shown the courage to speak out and denounce the Hindu nazis, the government and also the judiciary, they would have been dubbed "controversial" and made to face the wrath of the ruling class to which they belonged. Anybody who challenges the ruling class in India is dubbed "controversial" which in India is the other name for truth. The two "great historians" wanted to be in the good books of the rulers and thereby sacrificed the truth. How can we call those who are a party to perversion of history as historians?

India is full of such dishonest intellectuals — noisy, boisterous, bombastic, boastful and bogus. And anybody and everybody in India calls himself an intellectual. And such braggarts are front-paged so that the menace they create shall silence the simpletons. These intellectual prostitutes are persons with no conscience but factories that produce knowledge *sharbats.* And their numbers are increasing. The Hindu Nazi Bharatiya Janata Party (BJP) has its own captive knowledge managers. What happened to our marxists, red-hot communist intellectuals? They also belong to the same *jati.*

Chief obstacle for social change: Honest intellectuals are a dying species if not dead. No daily paper or periodical offers them a column. Not even their name appears in print. As for TV, it has nothing to do with intellectual interests. It is all glamour, beauty, fashion, sex, scandals, crimes, sports — entertainment, eternal entertainment. In other words, TV in India is an entertainer of the elite who are none but our "middle class" which is the other name to hide the identity of this class who are none but the upper castes.

Intellectuals and intellectuals alone can lead a society. Only such a society led by its fiery band of intellectuals can be a healthy society. But, alas, the Indian pond of intellectuals has dried up. It is barren. India has become a vast intellectual Sahara desert.

Nay, the Indian intellectuals have become a band of counter-revolutionaries. And today they are the chief obstacle for any social change.

Indore press conference: This writer was a newspaper reporter for 25 years. And attended scores of press conferences. A press conference is essentially meant to put questions and seek clarification on a given subject for which the press meet is called. With deep regret we have to say that even in metropolitan cities where "big newspaper people" work, a press conference invariably turns into a brawl if the person who calls the press meet happens to be from a section opposed to the interests of the ruling upper castes.

As we hold such press people in utter contempt (exceptions prove the rule), we seldom hold a press meet. But at the height of the anti-Dalit upper caste agitation against Dr. Ambedkar's book, *Riddle of Rama & Krishna* (1995, Dalit Sahitya Akademy), we were forced by our Dalit hosts at Indore to address a press meet at the Indore Press Club itself.

Hindu belief system: The press people, mostly upper castes, had come prepared for a fight with us and from the beginning we were under attack. We were not even allowed to distribute the press note prepared on the subject matter of the meet. The contention of every press reporter was that both the Hindu gods, Rama and Krishna, were "historical figures". When we asked a woman reporter to tell us which Indian history book said that, she asserted that every history book that she "studied" in her school and college had said this. All other reporters agreed. And the press meet ended in confusion and chaos with full abuse against us and Dr. Babasaheb Ambedkar.

And these are the type of journalists who abound in India — calling themselves intellectuals. This is the gutter our intellectuals are made of. That is why we very often say a Hindu believes in what he wants to believe.

A Hindu (upper caste) does not believe in rational thinking, scientific temper, logical arguments or facts of history. He believes in what is advantageous to his caste interest. Can such a class of people with a closed mind produce any intellectual? There was one: D.D. Kosambi.

Fraudmen called godmen: Take the case of Satya Sai Baba whom every paper in India continues to describe as *Bhagwan* (god) though every proof is there to say that he is a top class fraud. A team of scientists headed by the then Vice-

Chancellor of Bangalore University, Dr. H. Narasimhaiah, called gandhian by the upper castes, had proved that this Bhagwan could not "produce" anything larger than his fist could hold. But India's "top scientists" like S. Bhagwantam and Dr. Raja Ramanna are his devotees. How can such people be called scientists? This Sai Baba is facing serious murder charges and the court is seized with that but silenced by the corrupt rulers of the land and hushed up by the media. Hundreds of such fakes and frauds are parading in India as godmen and god women but India's media does not tear them to pieces and our "intellectuals" are silent devotees of these frauds. Even when the President and Prime Minister of India fall on the feet of these frauds our "intellectuals" are not agitated. And such intellectuals get all sorts of awards and rewards.

Why blame politicians: Our whole society has started stinking mainly because of the silence of our intellectuals. They are silent because they are a silent party to these frauds. Why blame politicians? Any corrupt politician like Jayalalita or P.V. Narasimha Rao can be simply fried in burning oil if only our intellectuals had been honest. These intellectuals' sole single preoccupation is protecting the status quo. Are we then wrong in calling them counter-revolutionaries?

So, there is no surprise that India's intellectuals constitute the fighting front of the counter-revolutionary movement sweeping India. They are pulling us back. India cannot be saved unless these counter-revolutionaries are first finished.

***Vastu* crackpots:** Look at our *Vastu* crackpots, the latest to dominate India's intellectual horizon, pushing the soothsayers, astrologers, tantriks, palmists and planet-gazers to the background. Premier scientific institutions are specialising in *Vastu Shastra*. How do you like that? When did this *Vastu* descend on this earth? Even ten years back, we have not heard of any such great architectural oracle. If *Vastu* was such a great scientific marvel it should have been an universal phenomenon. But the world outside India knows nothing of this great scientific discovery that has thrown out of job hundreds of architects. Quixotic quacks have taken over the field to frighten and browbeat the neo-rich who want to invest in construction activities by taking advantage of the building boom during P.V. Narasimha Rao's pro-upper caste rule when the Manmohan Singh miracle created hundreds of Harshad Mehtas and impoverished the country but bulged the belly of the rich.

Has any single "scientist" of India denounced them— the thugs and pindaris in the garb of *Vastu Shastra* specialists?

Stealing Western secrets: A society, if it has to grow on healthy lines, must be certainly a devotee of scientific temper. A scientist to qualify himself as a scientist must essentially possess scientific temper. A person without a scientific temper cannot be called a scientist even if he heads a scientific institute These suited and booted scientists have never seen a scientific laboratory but they are always found in the corridors of power or *ashrams* of godmen.

That is why India has not received a single Nobel Prize in science after independence. How can any scientist in India get a Nobel Prize when they mostly belong to one class and one caste?

A scientist has to be an iconoclast, an idol-breaker, an outspoken critic of men and matter.

But here we have a scientist, Dr. Raja Ramanna, a devotee of godman called Satya Sai Baba who is charged with murdering seven persons in his bedroom and "producing" wristwatches and rings after secretly buying them in the market. How can this fellow be called a scientist?

Naturally, these bogus scientists got stomach-ache when a

Muslim, Dr. A.P.J Abdul Kalam, got Hindu India's highest award of *Bharat Ratna*. Kalam is not only a Muslim but a dark-looking Tamil Dalit convert to Islam from Tamil Nadu. Kalam getting *Bharat Ratna* created so much of heart-burning among our heaven-born *vaidik* scientists who normally steal some Western scientific papers and claim it as their thesis.

Scientist's false claim: One such agriculture scientist, Dr. M.S. Swaminathan, a "big name" in India, was once caught red-handed for bagging the Magsasay Award by making a false claim that a dwarf wheat produced by him contained more protein content than milk. When the fraud was discovered, the *vaidik* vampire quickly dispatched him off on a foreign assignment until his theft was forgotten by the country. He has now come back with great many dazzling "discoveries" to bamboozle the gullible. The fraud of this "scientist" was brought to light by an inquiry committee then headed by the retired Chief Justice of the Supreme Court, Justice Gajendragadkar.

Intellectual wasteland: It is no wonder, therefore, that the youth is fed up with India. Its idealism is set on fire. And that is why hundreds of our talented youngsters do not even return to India after getting foreign education. A distinguished scientist, Dr. Hargobind Khorana, who had come to his motherland in search of a job in 1966, had to return broken-hearted back to Cambridge. This was the experience of a scientist who was destined to win a Nobel Prize. It is this desperate situation that made V.B. Kulkarni, a noted columnist, to complain:

> "This is an intellectual wasteland with only a few cases dotting the arid expanse".
>
> (*Indian Express*, Jan.10. 1974).

Science came to India almost by accident and its very survival here is a sheer accident. Because science is foreign to Hindu ethos - vagueness of time, the multi-valued truth, inevitability of *karma* and re-incarnation, the ethics of conformity and the morbid search for security with singular blandness.

Scientist defends *karma* theory: The best example of this inherent contradiction in the Indian scientific community's double-dealing is found in the statement of Dr. M.S. Swaminathan, who, as the then Director-General of ICAR and the topmost Indian agricultural scientist who got the Magsaysay Award, said:

> "The most fascinating part of Hindu thought relates to evolution — *karma. Karma* has been a much maligned concept, but in a sense it provides opportunities for moral growth and perfection. Being a dynamic concept, with no particular end point, it provides opportunities for correction of mistakes and continuous improvements. Avoiding the once-for-all alternatives of heaven and hell, it urges men to strive towards self-realiziation."
>
> (*Illustrated Weekly,* Nov.17, 1974).

As a Brahmin, Dr. Swaminathan found nothing wrong with the *karma* theory that killed the spirit of revolt among the suffering masses.

One of the curious and elemental features of Hindu ethos is the conceptual enormity of time which permeats the society enabling even our scientists to be quite vague about time. Time became a sort of timelessness, giving a cloak to hide their imprecise and impractical approach. Indian scientists have hardly attempted to question the theory of *karma* and reincarnation — which together provide the sheet anchor of continuity and stability to a highly disparate and unequal social order.

Indian Goebbels: There is no wonder that in such circumstances, our scientists in search of security, publicity and *kushy* jobs resort to such dubious methods of making false and exaggerated claims, stealing scientific data and downright interpolation.

Dr. Swaminathan himself became the target of criticism by top Western scientists regarding his "exaggerated claims" on *sharbati sonara* ,a new strain of dwarf wheat, for which he got the international award.

The Sarvodaya leader of the "Total Revolution" fame, Jayaprakash Narayan's weekly, *Everyman*'s ((Dec.15, 1974) had come out with the following startling disclosure on this fake scientist:

> "Parliamentarians have dubbed Dr. Swaminathan as a public relations scientist and the Indian version of the master German propagandist, Goebbels. But these epithets have not deterred him from continuing to indulge in falsehoods... The point now is not whether Swaminathan spoke lies repeatedly to go up the bureaucratic ladder. It has been established in the *New Scientist* article that he published false data".

The *Everyman's* had then reproduced the article published in the Nov.7, 1974 issue of the prestigious British monthly, *New Scientist*, to make the Indian policy-makers aware of the reputation enjoyed by Swaminathan in the international sphere.

Total failure of "Green Revolution": The *New Scientist* article by Joseph Hanlon quoted internationally reputed scientists including Norman Borlough to disprove the claims of Swaminathan and expose his intellectual taxidermy.

The special technical advisory panel to the Gajendragadkar Committee which went into the affairs of the Indian Council of Agriculture Research then made a devastating comment on the entire scientific community in general.

> "The phenomenal is not confined to ICAR". It continued: "Barring minor exceptions, it pervades the entire scientific and academic community in this country. At the root of it is the greed for bureaucratic power and love of comfortable life which afflicts this class".
>
> (*Everyman's* Dec. 15, 1974).

It is a misfortune that scientists in India, with the handful of exceptions, have become a buttering lot. To please Jawaharlal Nehru, who believed in gigantism against M.K. Gandhi's concept of "small is beautiful", they built the "modern temples" — all of which turned out to be white elephants. A chain of "national laboratories" were established and millions of rupees went down the drain. The much-publicised "Green Revolution" proved to be a total failure. But our scientists are enjoying a kushy life with foreign travels, attending seminars and getting photographed with ministers. Many of them have turned semi-politicians. And to keep their secrets, all the scientific research wings of the government is out of bound for SC/ST "reserved sector" people.

Science can grow only under clash of ideas, but in India no scientist questions the traditional ideas. Questioning is never permitted in Hindu India. The process of dialogue, confrontation, clash and conflict promotes a need to reject some of the old and outworn ideas and traditions which are not compatible or cannot be modified and co-exist with new ones. In the process of developing new set of values our ethos changes. This leads to growth. But in Hindu India our scientists are holding on to the old values — not even trying to re-interpret them. Their heart is in America with their feet in India — copying Western manners but never giving up their cross-thread.

Thus the Indian scientific community is totally indifferent to the widespread social injustice, economic disparities and religious exploitation that engulf the society. They are cool. It has paid heavy dividends at least to some of them to keep mum — privileges and perquisites in return for abdication of our right to assert the reconstruction of our value system that has outlived the social purposes.

Never before the truth about Indian scientific research has

been told in all bluntness as by Dr. S, Bhagawantham, a former Scientific Adviser to the Government of India, when he said that 90% of the present-day research is "thoroughly irrelevant" to the economic needs of the country. (*Deccan Herald* Jan.11, 1975). This makes it clear how our ivory tower scientists are wasting their time on window-dressing, totally cut off from the social environs. The opinion expressed in the 70's is further confirmed when research and development (R&D) is totally neglected not only in government sector but also in private sector.

Have we ever heard of a cooperative effort in the scientific field in Hindu India? This is because the *karma* theory, reincarnation and individual salvation never encourage the value of cooperative effort — either in scientific or for that matter in any other sphere in Hindu India: Hence collective effort is unheard of in the scientific field. Under such all-pervading darkness we see not even a glimmer of hope for science in Hindu India. So, the best of the lot take refuge in foreign countries. Those who linger inside Hindu India are by and large frustrated and disillusioned.

Indian doctors, engineers and scientists run away to foreign countries not only to escape from the rigours of Hindu India but also to seek a happy life which they can never hope to get inside India. After all, patriotism and nationalism will not fill their belly.

Merit, my foot: Why do Indian scientists rarely achieve international eminence? This is mainly because in India the "merit" goes with one's *jati* (V.T. Rajshekar: *Merit, My Foot,* Dalit Sahitya Akademy, 1996). A team of researchers in Chicago University, after completing a 5-year study of some 120 eminent people from all walks of life, found that such eminence is not simply born. It is made. Nobody is a born genius. A genius is like a tree. A seed grows into a mighty tree only if it has the proper environment to grow. Bad weather, pest, a grazing cow or some such hostile atmosphere may nip it in the bud itself. A genius is made by parents, family, society around, education system, proper nourishment. The Chicago University study revealed that potential eminence in individuals is not uncommon. The great majority of them go unnoticed, unrecognised. Given the right conditions they can become eminent too.

Dr. Babasaheb Ambedkar was one such genius. He was a product of the British Raj. Had he lived in "independent" India of today, the country would not have seen a Babasaheb. "Independent" India produced no second Babasaheb. It produced only pigmies.

Dr. Buckminister Fuller, father of geodesic dome and many other inventions, says:

> "Genius can get born only when you have outspoken opinions about everything, from education to the essence of universe".

Chief Justice remark: The management guru, Lee Iacocca, attributed his roaring success to his parents. He said: "It is amazing how in a free society you can become as great as you want to be".

But is our Indian society free? Barring two or three who did not last even 2-3 years, every Prime Minister of India has been a Brahmin. The Chief Justice of the Supreme Court, Justice A.S. Anand (1999), when pointed out by President of India K.R. Narayanan that the Supreme Court had not even a single Dalit on its bench, said no Dalit had the merit to reach that status. The Chief Justice had the support of the India's intellectual class. Otherwise, he would not have got the courage to make such a serious racist remark against a community. India's "intellectual class" did not protest against the remarks of the Chief Justice.

We, as a writer and journalist, come under the category of

intellectuals. And during our 25 years in daily newspaper journalism and later as Editor we had occasions to interact with many journalists, writers and such intellectuals. But our experience with these intellectuals has not been so cosy.

As a Dalit journalist we fight for the cause of justice, truth and freedom which are denied to over 85% of India's oppressed. And in this struggle we have waged, first in English dailies and then as Editor, we have hardly found an "intellectual" who was prepared to go with us.

Magic & monopoly of English: This is mainly because of the situation peculiar to Indian society - namely the deathless institution called the caste system which builds a wall between man and man. When it comes to caste there is no free flow of opinion or judgement.

Writers and intellectuals to be qualified as intellectuals in this country have to be essentially English-knowing. And in India to reach the status of reading, writing and speaking English is a rare privilege. And this privilege is reserved mainly for the upper castes, and that too the heaven-born *vaidiks.* An ascending order of reverence and descending degree of contempt. This is the meaning of Hindu caste.

English is the privilege of the rich. And in India the rich are mainly the upper castes. The institution of caste confers privileges on the high-born and because of these privileges, the high-born acquire status which comes from their wealth which affords them to get English education which in turn brings them status.

In other words, the upper castes are mainly the monopoly-holders of English education and hence entitled to be called intellectuals. And this class of intellectuals has its interests exactly opposite to that of India's Untouchables, Tribals, Backward Castes and other oppressed comprising over 85% of the population of India. The institution of caste has put the

15% upper castes (Hindus) in opposition to the 85% non-Hindu original inhabitants. So, both class-wise and caste-wise the two are hostile to each other. The former are the rulers and oppressors of the other section.

Who stands for the underdog: The intellectuals of India should have naturally stood by the oppressed if they are entitled to be called intellectuals and hence defenders of freedom, justice and truth. But they are not. And if there are any exceptions to this rule, we are not aware of them.

When this is the fact, what right they have to be called intellectuals? Have they proved to be the scourge and scavenger of the society? Are they ready to suffer and sacrifice for the underdog?

Some upper caste intellectuals "confess" that they stand for the underdog. If so, where is the evidence? There is no such thing as "private intellectuals". A writer has to write and whatever that he or she writes is public document. How can one say he is a "private intellectual"?

Intellectuals will have to use all the weapons at their command — talking, writing, teaching, appearing on TV and any other means. And what they do must be publicly recognisable. But in India we have no such "intellectual" who can be recognised as a selfless fighter, the scourge and scavenger of the society. Because the moment an intellectual fights for the cause of freedom, truth and justice he or she immediately attracts the wrath of the rulers who happen to be his or her *jatwala*. And in India we have hardly any example of an intellectual defying his *jati*.

Take the case of B.V. Karanth. Reports of his fight with a woman at Bhopal and causing her serious burn injuries was big news. Vibha Mishra, if the name is correct, was about to die of burns. But nothing happened to B.V. Karanth. He was defended by all "fellow intellectuals". R.K. Hegde, then Chief Minister of

Karnataka, held a press conference, defending his *jatwala* and calling him innocent. Justice in this country goes with one's *jati.*

As per this logic neither Jayalalitha nor P.V. Narasimha Rao are called corrupt despite mountains of evidence. And both these political leaders have been giving lectures on justice and truth and newspapers have been devoting columns of space for their orations. This is the depth of the gutter to which our journalism has descended. The words may be strong but they are true.

That is why India has not produced a Jean-Paul Sartre or a Betrand Russel.

An honest intellectual has to challenge not only the society, its ruling class but also his or her own family and even the spouse. He or she had to be ruthlessly honest and prepared to face criminal charges, sedition or any other section in the Criminal Procedure Code or Indian Penal Code. Not even the Terrorist Act (TADA) can silence the intellectual.

Question of faith: He shall question everybody, confront everybody including the god. An intellectual is a genius, perhaps a "mad" person from conventional standards.

When the intellectual defies god himself, naturally he has to be an atheist. But in India our intellectuals are not only superstitious and all-out god-worshippers but even worshippers of godmen. To an intellectual nothing is dearer than justice and truth, human freedom and knowledge.

We remember very well those days when we formed in Bangalore a Committee to Investigate the (alleged) Miracles of India's richest godman, Satya Sai Baba. Bangalore is the home of many scientific institutions with scores of scientists. But not only no scientist came forward in our mission but they put forward all sorts of obstacles and put out false reports in the press, engineered an agitation against the committee, defended the godman, (who later was charged with murdering seven devotees in his bedroom), and finally saw to it that the chairman of the committee was dismissed as vice-chancellor of Bangalore University itself.

We were then in the *Indian Express* and using our position we wrote personal letters to many "eminent scientists". None responded and a couple of them who replied, evaded the question. Some even suggested that we should not question the "faith" of devotees of the godman.

Scientists believing in faith? What is faith? Faith in superstition, miracles, sooth-saying, astrology and such other fake things?

That is why India cannot produce honest intellectuals because such intellectuals are essentially bound by their caste and have no courage to defy their caste. Caste can produce only corruption and no corruption is a greater crime than caste corruption. And the first charge against India's intellectuals is caste corruption. Their values are marketable, easily purchased, all professions reduced to pursuit of easy money, quick success, eternal pleasure — all at somebody else's expense.

How to manufacture an intellectual: The moment a newspaper calls a person as intellectual, publishes his bullshit speech, prints his picture that person becomes an "eminent intellectual". P.V. Narasimha Rao, the living Chanakya, who came out to be called India's most corrupt Prime Minister and promoted his *jatwalas* to amass wealth by hook or crook, was being described in our brahminical media as a scholar and intellectual. Such is the specimen of intellectuals that India has.

An intellectual is one who promotes revolutionary ideas that must contribute to social change. What is the contribution of this Chanakya? Nobody knows. And yet the country's brahminical newspapers go on applying the adjective to these political leaders. And our intellectuals have no objection. Perhaps this appelation goes with a certain caste. Yes. The tragedy of India is "merit" goes with one's caste and our intellectuals are the greatest upholders of caste-based "merit".

Parade of instant intellectuals: What is the social vision of this Chanakya? The public knows him as casteist, extremely dishonest, cunning, crafty, manipulative and anti-social. And yet he is called an intellectual. It is only such anti-social elements who are called intellectuals. And when the ruling class describes one as intellectual and puts out columns of their speeches, they are sold as intellectuals. While the fact is they are anti-social and corrupt to the core. What future such a society can have where anti-social elements are paraded as intellectuals?

India has hundreds of such hired agents of information industry — instant intellectuals.

We have said that a society's progress depends upon its honest intellectuals. Hired agents can only take the society back and India having gone back, has virtually hit the wall. And there is no place to go further back. And yet India's ruling class is not ashamed and not one "intellectual" it propped up has the courage to speak out the truth.

US defeat in Gulf War: To such intellectual prostitutes, their business of prostitution has become more important than the survival of the society. India has become a vast intellectual Sahara desert.

The "media industry" has hoisted a number of such intellectual prostitutes and they have plenty of customers, handful of money and a kushy life.

During the first Gulf War (1990), we were perhaps the only

journal in India to condemn the US for invading Iraq. We editorially criticised the US and stood by Saddam Hussein. We even predicted that Saddam would come out unscathed and the US would get defeated.

Indian "intellectuals" who read our writings in 1990 called us mad and said within a week Iraq would be pounded and powdered.

The intellectuals proved wrong and we proved right. The London *Economist*(May 1, 1999 p. 86-87) reviewed two books, both by Western writers fully supporting our stand. (Andrew Cockburn and Patrick Cockburn, *Out of the Ashes — The Resurrection of Saddam Hussein*, Harper Collins, 1999) and the other one by Scott Ritter, a former UN weapons inspector (*End Game: Solving the Iraq Problem*, Simon & Schuster).

It was a very difficult period in the history of our journal. The popular mood engineered by the zionist-controlled world media made everybody believe that Iraq would be finished like a fly. But an intellectual who has a deep insight into social forces will think, ponder and come to right conclusions without falling a prey to the cacophony of the media. Only an exceptionally brilliant person can escape the media bombardment and brainwashing. An honest intellectual can certainly steer clear of the flood and swim against the current. India had none and all of them were carried away by the Western propaganda.

The same thing was repeated during the second Gulf War (1998). Once again we backed Saddam. We took a tremendous risk. Support to justice and truth is always a risky business.

Sikhs struggle for self-determination: The two Gulf Wars were not the only occasion. We faced a similar situation in our support to the Sikh struggle for self-determination (1982-1986). It cost us a lot including our arrest under the dreaded Terrorist

Act (TADA), hand-cuffed and taken all the way from Bangalore to Chandigarh.

And at that time (1986), the country's journalists and intellectuals in general heaved a sigh of relief that this thorn (*Dalit Voice*) in their flesh was at last removed and destroyed. Upper caste journalists in the Bangalore Press Club downed a double-peg when they heard our arrest under TADA. They congratulated each other saying that this menace would never come back to Bangalore as there was no bail under the TADA. And even if he did come back, he would be back with some broken limbs.

As intellectuals, it is our duty to be on the side of the weak, the persecuted and the unrepresented. The Sikhs had all these qualifications.

Their demand for self-determination (not secession) was as old as India's freedom movement. They gladly opted to stay with India though an assurance of an autonomous Sikh homeland within Pakistan was given by Jinnah, the Father of Pakistan. Yet they opted for India and the Indian leaders gave them all the promises which were broken the moment India's upper caste rulers gained "independence" (1947) and started imposing their upper caste rule.

Sant Bhindranwale, perhaps the only Sikh religious leader (a Jat), was the first to declare a war against the Hindu rulers. And Mrs. Indira Gandhi, the then Prime Minister, guided by her upper caste advisers dubbed the Sikh movement led by Sant Bhindranwale as secessionist, anti-national and terrorist, sent the Indian Army itself (1984) to wage a war against India's proudest and bravest sons (Sikhs), and killed over 4,000 of them in the Sikh's holiest temple (Amritsar) including women and children. (*Oppression in Punjab*, Citizens for Democracy, foreword by Justice V.M. Tarkunde and preface by George Fernandes, 1985, pp.130).

Phoolan Devi called dacoit: No intellectual can tolerate the use of Army for internal purposes. And that too against a Sikh religious congregation inside their holiest temple and killing hundreds of women and children.

"Blue Star Operation", as it was named by the Army, was described by the press as the greatest tragedy that fell upon India after the 1947 partition. But the Hindus of India celebrated the occasion and said the Sikhs deserved it. India's national papers had put out all sorts of false reports prejudicing the minds of innocent readers.

We simply wept when we came to know that the Army marched into Golden Temple and butchered the Sikhs in cold blood. But our journalist colleagues laughed and said that we were mad. A Sikh IAS officer of the Karnataka cadre, Sardar Chiranjivi Singh, who took part in a silent march of the Bangalore Sikhs to mourn the death of their fellow Sikhs, was punished by the upper caste bureaucrats and one journalist who came to the rescue of this innocent and also upright official had to suffer and finally he had to quit Karnataka itself having been given no promotion. This is the type of intellectuals we have in India. They would not stand by the weak, the unrepresented and the persecuted.

Phoolan Devi, a poor Backward Caste woman, who was raped non-stop by dozens of upper caste Thakurs in her village, was continuously being described as a dacoit by the press just because she joined a gang of dacoits to wreak vengeance on these Thakurs. The same press people who call Phoolan Devi a dacoit, do not apply the same description to a bigger dacoit, Jayalalita, because she is their *jatwali.*

Though India has scores of women's organisations, no organisation was prepared to take up her case. Phoolan was sent to jail and for four years she was tortured in the jail. But India's upper caste women's organisations hated her and treated her with contempt though she can be easily described as India's greatest human rights leader for women. India's intellectuals despised her but the unlettered innocent masses respected Phoolan Devi and elected her to Parliament.

To speak up and fight for the cause of the wretched of the earth like Phoolan it needs steady realism, tremendous rational energy. And above all that courage that comes out of conviction. Indian upper castes lack it because caste blinds their thinking. They are a set of dead wood. That is why India has not produced a Voltair.

War against Islam: No person can remain an island. No honest intellectual can remain an island. He has to be a citizen of the whole world, not merely of his country or the society he belongs to.

When communication and travel revolution has made this universe a global village and banking or share market upset in Japan or Malaysia can send waves all over the world, an intellectual cannot say he is concerned only with his country.

When President Clinton ordered cruise missile attack on two poor Muslim countries — Afghanistan and Sudan — on Aug.22, 1998, it had world-wide repercussions. It was not merely an aggression against two Muslim countries but a declaration of war against Islam itself. There was no proof of the Saudi millionaire revolutionary Osma Bin Laden's involvement in the bombing of US embassies in Nairobi and Dar-es-Salam earlier. Bin Laden had officially denied his hand. Yet Clinton ordered the attack killing thousands of innocent Muslims. Barring the usual camp-followers of the US, the world leader of the White Western racists, like UK, France, Canada etc., there was world-wide protest against Clinton's thoughtless action. India's upper caste rulers naturally went with their White Western Aryan counterparts. But was there any honest intellectual protest against the Indian support to US aggression? Some "intellectuals" when asked reasons for their silence said: Why should we get embroiled in a dispute between US and some Islamic terrorists?"

The question is simple and straight. Can an intellectual sit back in silence when blatant violations of a country's sovereignty are taking place with impunity disregarding all norms set by the United Nations itself? What proof US has that Bin Laden has ordered the bombing of US embassies? Even if it had any proof, the US is duty-bound to complain to the UN, explore normal diplomatic channels instead of resorting to direct armed attack on sovereign-states like Afghanistan, Sudan and Iraq.

Prejudice against Muslims: But the world of intellectuals in general and the Indian in particular kept mum; rather they silently enjoyed the killing just because the victims happened to be Muslims.

Prejudice against Islam and Muslim blinded our intellectuals. They did not view the victims as human beings. The death and devastation may not be inside India but when US can behave like a highway robber what prevents it from making a similar attack on India alleging that some Indian Muslims are involved in the conspiracy?

This is where we find fault with our intellectuals. There is nothing like "Indian intellectuals", Chinese intellectuals and that of Chile. All those styling themselves as intellectuals are world citizens. No intellectual can remain an island.

But in a situation like the two Gulf Wars and the US attack on Afghanistan and Sudan, the intellectuals of the world in general and those in India became blind with prejudice. Their hatred of Islam made the American journalists take refuge in "nationalism". They suddenly became "nationalists" and found that as Americans they have a duty to defend America and the American government actions. They found nothing wrong in US action against Saddam Hussain twice and the subsequent air attacks on two Muslim countries. The intellectuals' "nationalist" duties made them manufacture lies that sounded truthful and the war and violence on innocents respectable.

As far as we can remember, *Dalit Voice* broke through this stereotype and condemned the US aggression and defended Saddam Hussein.

During the first Gulf War, "national" dailies in India put out mountains of lies, just reprinting the Western newspaper reports predicting that Saddam would be crushed and finished within days. Nothing happened.

Saddam grew stronger and the US was forced to resort to a second attack and once again the same lies were repeated. And once again the journalists were forced to eat their own words. Saddam remained confident and fully in saddle. The US mad dog ate dust. But our intellectuals remain shameless even when they have all proved wrong. A person wanting to be called an intellectual cannot suffer from prejudice.

Babasaheb on Indian journalism: Dr. Babasaheb Ambedkar once said:

> Journalism in India was once a profession. It has how become a trade. It has no more function than the manufacture of soap. It does not regard itself as the responsible adviser of the public. To give the news uncoloured by any motive, to present a certain view of public policy which it believes to be for the good of the community, to correct and chastise without fear all those, no matter how high, who have chosen a wrong or barren path, is not regarded by journalism in India its first or foremost duty. To accept a hero and worship him has become its principal duty. Under it, news gives place to sensation, reasoned opinion to unreasoning passion, appeal to the minds

of responsible people to appeal to emotions of the irresponsible".

(Ranade, Gandhi & Jinnah, 1978, Bheem Patrika Publications, Jalandhar -3, p.39),

Babasaheb made these observations in 1943 — seven years before India became "independent". The state of journalism in India on the eve of the 21st century can be well imagined.

Clash of civilisations: Prof. Samuel Huntington of Harvard University is a big name in American intellectual circles. And his book, *Clash of Civilisations* (Penguin Books 1996) is considered a prophetic prediction on the shape of the things to come.

But what type of a prophet is Huntington who equates religion with "civilisation" and takes over the job of a historian? As a Jew and a White Western American he is giving vent to his hatred of Islam and Muslim. This makes him camouflage his hatred and describe his call for all-out war against Islam as a "Clash of civilisations". Yet this hate-mongering fellow was hailed a great intellectual giant. This is the tragedy as the 20th century is nearing its end.

Huntington's thesis of "civilisational war" and its total endorsement by the White Western society and its Aryan counterpart in India make us doubt the honesty of intellectuals in US. Barring Naom Chomsky, Edward Said and a couple of others, even such a great country like the US — which wants to lead the world after defeating Islam, China, Blacks and the Browns of the world — is fast becoming intellectually bankrupt.

Clinton's sex scandal: Even when the entire Arab press put out reports that Clinton's sex scandal was part of a zionist conspiracy to force Clinton to get tough with Islamists, the American, European and Indian media kept silent. Monica Lewinsky, a Jewish girl, was set up after the zionists came to know Clinton's weakness. As the zionists control the American media, business and even the government, they could bully Clinton even to the extent of making him yield. The cruise missile attack on two Muslim countries proved that Clinton yielded though ultimately he came out unscathed.

Why no intellectual in America brought out all these inner secrets? Even if all these things are not 100% facts, at least there should have been an honest discussion on the subject. If the American public opinion survey (which is again manufactured) has excused Clinton, why was he crucified? Is it not a clear proof of a conspiracy behind Clinton's sex scandals?

Thousands, if not millions, of Muslims were killed in Algeria. But why no Western human rights organisations, not even the most famous Amnesty International, sent any fact-finding team to find out the truth? Is it because those killed happened to be all Muslims and the killing had the Western (read French) blessings?

The West is so much concerned about "human rights violations" in China, Malaysia and Indonesia but not in Algeria, Bosnia, Kosovo, Sudan, Iraq. Because all those killed are Muslims. Inside the US, its own Black nationals are ill-treated and hated by its White rulers. Why no Western human rights organisation points out these double-standards? Why India's intellectuals are also silent on this?

The Untouchables of India form about 20% of India's population. Together with Tribals (10%), they constitute a third of India — which means more than the population of whole Europe. Such a vast population is scattered not only all over India but in every village of India and urban centres.

It is a common knowledge that it is this 30% of the population which is at the bottom of the society. But is there any concern, discussion, debate or objective reporting or articles on this vital segment? On the other hand, the media is full of irresponsible if not prejudicial reporting and editorial comments. This is intellectual dishonesty. Senior journalists, editors, writers, academicians have either prejudiced opinion on this section or just plain unconcern. Even the Supreme Court of India in a recent judgment said Untouchables cannot become super speciality doctors as they lacked "merit", and described reservations as anti-national. Our intellectuals had no objection to such a racist remark by the highest court of the land.

Human Rights Watch report: Even India's government-sponsored National Human Rights Commission has not undertaken a study on the denial of human rights to this single largest segment of India. We find the same prejudice against Muslims who form another 15% of the population.

Human Rights Watch had to send a team to India to unravel these hidden Hindu secrets about "Hindu tolerance", gandhian non-violence, compassion and milk of human kindness flowing all over India. A report brought out by this New York-based organisation (*Broken People — Caste Violence Against India's Untouchables*- 1999, pp.300, Human Rights Watch, New York) — first of its kind — was completely blacked out in the press.

You cannot entirely blame the press though it has a role to mould the reading habit of a society. The problem with India is its English-knowing population which being mainly upper caste is really not interested in reading anything not tasteful. The Untouchables are hated and hence the media keeps out the Untouchables.

Intellectuals lead a society: This is the state of the intellectual class in India. Rearing and guiding of a society — whether it is Indian, Chinese, Brazilian or Kenyan — always depends upon its intellectual class. Intellectuals and intellectuals alone can lead a society. But such intellectuals will have to be honest. All those societies led by honest intellectuals have progressed and prospered. But India has lagged if not rotted because it is led by its dishonest intellectuals. If India is what it is today the credit goes entirely to our intellectuals. Not politicians. Blaming everything on our politicians is the mischief of this failed intellectual class.

This intellectual class boasts about its hoary past, "glorious civilisation" and how its Hindu civilisation "survived" despite numerous invasions and onslaughts of hostile religions. But these intellectuals do not want to consider the question on what plane does it survive. The Indian society is not only not living but merely existing — neither living nor dead. Our intellectuals cannot take comfort in the fact that India is the only country surviving since centuries despite all odds. But what is the quality of this survival? Amoeba is also surviving on the sea side. But how many people trample upon it while walking on the sea shore? Indians too have survived like this amoeba. Kicked by every invader, the Hindu's life is a life of continuous defeat. India's intellectuals are blind to this plain fact.

Such a poverty of thought in our "intellectual" class has made us a laughing stock all over the world. In other words, the failure of India is the failure of its intellectual class — not its politicians, not its businessmen or its bureaucrats. We put the blame mainly on its intellectuals who are dishonest.

Cause of intellectual's fall: Dr. Babasaheb Ambedkar attributes this steep decline, fall and slow death of India's intellectual class to the fact that in India, the intellectuals came to be identified with a particular caste:-

> Buddha realized that for a person to give a true lead to society and be its trustworthy guide he must be intellectually free and further, which is more important, to be intellectually free he must not have private property. An elite charged with the care

of his private property must fail to discharge his duty of leading and guiding Society along the right road. Buddha therefore took care to include in the Code of discipline for the Bhikshus a rule prohbiting a Bhikshu from holding private property. In the Vedic order of Brahmins there was no such prohibition. A Brahmin was free to hold property. This difference produced a profound difference on the character and outlook of the Buddhist Bhikshu and the Vedic Brahmin. The Bhikshus formed an intellectual class. The Brahmins formed on the other hand merely an educated class. There is a great difference between an intellectual class and an educated class. An intellectual class has no limitations arising out of any affiliations to any class or to any interest. An educated Class on the other hand is not an intellectual class although it has cultivated its intellect. The reason is that its range of vision and its sympathy to a new ideology is circumscribed by its being identified with the interest of the class with which it is affiliated.

The Brahmins from the very beginning therefore were inclined to be a purely educated class, enlightened but selfish. This evil in the Vedic order of Brahmins was extreme by the changes made in the old Vedic system. The right of the Brahmins to rule and the grant of special privileges and immunities made them more selfish, and induced in them the desire to use their education not for the advancement of learning for the use of their community and against the advancement of society.

All their energy and their education has been spent in maintaining their own privileges against the good of the public. It has been the boast of many Hindu authors that the civilization of India is the most ancient civilization in the world. They will insist that there was no branch of knowledge in which their ancestors were not the pioneers. Open a book like "The Positive Background of Hindu Sociology" by Prof. Benoy Kumar Sarkar, or a book like "The Positive Sciences of the Ancient Hindus" by Dr. Brajendranath Seal one is overwhelmed with data touching upon the knowledge their ancestors had about various scientific subjects. From these books it would appear that the ancient Indians knew astronomy, astrology, biology, chemistry, mathematics, medicine, minerology, physics and in the view of the mass of people even aviation. All this may be very true.

> The important question is not how the ancient Indians discovered these positive sciences. The important question is why did the ancient Indians cease to make any progress in the sciences in which they were the pioneers? This sudden arrest in the progress of science in ancient India is as astounding as it is deplorable. In the scientific world India occupies a position which even if it be first among the primitive is certainly last among the civilized nation. How did it happen that a people who began the work of scientific progress stopped, halted on the way, left in its incohate and incomplete condition? This is a question that needs to be considered and answered, not what the ancient Indians knew.
>
> There is only one answer to the question and it is a very simple answer. In ancient India the Brahmins were the only educated class. They were also the Class which was claiming to be above all others. Buddha disputed their claim for supremacy and declared a war on the Brahmins. The Brahmins acted as an Educated Class — as distinguished from an intellectual class — would act under the circumstances. It abandoned all pursuits and engaged itself in defending the claim of supremacy and the social, economic and political interests of its class.Instead of writing books on Science, the Brahmins undertook to write Smritis. Here is an explanation why the progress of science in India became arrested. Brahmins found it more important and more imperative to write Smritis to repel the Buddhist doctrine of social equality.
>
> (*Babasaheb Ambedkar Writings & Speeches, Vol.3, p. 322-23,* Maharashtra Govt. Publication, 1987*)*.

Dr. Babasaheb Ambedkar's verdict is perfect and final. Brahmins of India, he said, produced any number of learned people but not a single intellectual. Right from Budha, Mahavira, Guru Nanak, Sant Ravidas, Mahatma Phule, Vivekananda, Sri Narayana Guru, Periyar E.V. Ramaswamy, Dr. B.R. Ambedkar, Dr. R.M. Lohia, who are all credited with bringing about social change, were all non-Brahmins. Even M.K. Gandhi. Dr. Ambedkar, therefore, was right.

Pigmies & pea nuts: When we were in the *Indian Express* and earlier in the *Deccan Herald*, we had the pleasure of working under giants like Frank Moreas, Pothan Joseph etc. Such titans are no more. Pigmies and peanuts have taken over the world of journalism. If anybody wants to test this charge, they can walk into the house of any journalist and see his library (if at all he has one) and the type of books he reads. The best test is our press clubs beginning with the Press Club of India in Delhi. Journalists' main preoccupation in all these press clubs is drinking, playing cards, gossiping and racketeering. No intellectual discussion takes place. Intellectual pursuits do not pay. If you are an intellectual, you are called a bloody fool.

Hope in women journalists: The entry of women into this male sanctum sanctorum is a great relief. The fair sex is also fair in its judgement. They are not so prejudiced and do not yield to corruption. The oppressed Indians have more hope in women journalists.

Libraries are dying not only in press clubs but also in our colleges and universities. In our college days, we used to find our professors buried in books in libraries. But such prestigious libraries are today gathering dust. Go to JNU or Madras University or any other prestigious university library in India. You will weep on seeing the state of these libraries. Book shops are closing, dying. Calcutta's prestigous College Street has become a commercial centre. When intellectuals die what future is there for that society?

What is this "middle class": Marxists at least had some corner for intellectuals — once upon a time. When marxism itself died, where can we find intellectuals? India has become a vast intellectual Sahara desert.

Indian journalists have popularized a new name, "middle class". Our urban-born, urban-bred and urban-educated journalists are not mad in coining this new phrase. There is a method in their madness. The method is to hide the identity of this "middle class" — its class or (to be more precise) its caste character.

How honest is this class of journalists who have gate-crashed into this intellectual enclosure can be made out if we go into the content of this "middle class" which is the other word for India's ruling class — in other words upper castes. To hide this reality the media is using the new name "middle class". This class loves "democracy" because it suits its class interests. If this "middle class" had its way it would vote for military dictatorship. About 15% of the ruling upper castes belong to this enclosed "middle class". You go to any affluent market place you find this class crowding around and on a buying spree.

This cricket-crazy "middle class" is the most oppressive class because it comprises essentially the consumers of all wealth. They produce nothing. They peddle crass materialism and consumerism and suffer from total lack of concern for those outside its charmed circle.

Private education in "public school": If this 15% of the country's population had a choice, it would have conveniently elimated the rest. So, the most serious threat posed by this "middle class" is to the principle of social justice which gets the highest place in the Constitution of India. It is this 15% of the "middle class" that consumes the meat, milk, fruits, fish, liquor and all the luxury products and yet remains eternally dissatisfied despite endless holidays. It is this "middle class" which created the "public school system" so that it remains as the preserve of the private sector. The five-star culture, eternal entertainment is encouraged by this class. Vulgar display of wealth and involvement in all economic scandals are its speciality. It is this "middle class" that has taken to computer as an easy way to make money.

It is this "middle class" that has caused the disruption in the country's daily newspapers, forcing it to give priority to tripe and trivia. The *Times of India* in Delhi and Bangalore are specialising in publishing on front-pages what was considered indecent a decade or so ago. News has given place to views. Vidyadhar Date, whose report as the special correspondent of the *Times of India*, Bombay, on social and cultural issues used to be read with the great respect, are shunted to inside pages while fashion parades and sex scandals hit the front pages. The *Statesman,* once India's most prestigious English daily, lost its pre-eminent status because of the madness of this "middle class". The tragedy of India is that our "intellectuals" spring from this "middle class".

To conclude, it is not a lockout but a shutdown in India's intellectual sector. Our coffee house philosophers' pre-occupation with tripe and trivia has converted India into a vast intellectual Sahara desert. Such a disappearance of intellectuals should be a matter of serious concern. But no "intellectual" is worried because the class to which he or she belongs is the ruling class. And that is what worries us much more than India's descent to the level of a beggar nation.

****

ANNEXURE

India's "Intellectual" Prostitutes

(*Dalit Voice* Editorial of Dec. 1, 1985)

India's ruling class in its unending pursuit of pleasure sees corruption everywhere though those indulging in it are its own distinguished members. All those caught in the "spy scandal", bribery, tax evasion, smuggling, violating every law of the land belong only to this class. The poor forming 70% of the population are busy producing the wealth for the ruling class. When this ruling class talks of corruption it means only "money corruption" which is only a small part of the large world of corruption. The worst form of corruption is not "money corruption" but "intellectual corruption". In the "money corruption" only the bribe-giver and the taker are affected but in "intellectual corruption" the victim is the whole society. Nay. Generations after generations become sick. To fight and destroy Budhism and Jainism, the priestly class forged the scriptures. Forgery has been the national tradition with us, says V.R. Narla. "There is no parallel in the world history for such largescale literary fraud", he says referring to the change of the word *agre* in a hymn in the *Rig Veda* altered to *agne* by some "wretched priests". He also quotes Max Muller saying: "This is perhaps the most flagrant instance of what can be done by an unscrupulous priesthood". By this change of a word, thousands of non-Brahmins were killed. (V.R. Narla: *Poverty of Intellectualism in India*, Prasaranga, Mysore University - 570 012, Rs. 6, 1978, pp. 28). In Punjab, high caste Hindus disowned their own mother-tongue out of hatred against Sikhs. The Indian "communist" leadership preached brahminism in the name of Marxism. In the name of "merit" millions of Dalits and other persecuted minorities were denied opportunities to come up. Forgery to hide facts, dishonesty to promote their class/caste interests, keeping silent at crucial moments when facts become incovenient, describing an ass as race horse and vice-versa, character assassination of those working for social change are some of the favourite pastimes of these "intellectuals". Truth should not be said. Not only it should not be said, it should be suppressed at all times. Buttering and bum-licking, crawling when asked merely to bend are the great qualities of our "intellectuals" — writers, journalists, teachers, scientists, economists, historians, sociologists, artists. It is this class that is more corrupt than politicians, govt. servants and businessmen, though only the first two are often accused of being corrupt. If our politicians and govt. servants are corrupt, it is because our "intellectuals" are not exposing this corruption. "Money corruption" is a byproduct of "intellectual corruption".

The Indian "intellectuals" are a special breed. They are specialised in the art of swimming with the current. They get on well with anybody in power. But the one intellectual who showed tremendous guts was Arun Shourie who as the editor of the *Indian Express*, the country's largest English newspaper chain, fought Indira Gandhi tyranny and came to be hailed as the "Emergency hero". His "investigative reports" on the "Bhagalpur blinding case", his scathing attack on corruption resulting in the dismissal of Chief Minister Antulay made him the blue-eyed boy of Indian journalism, finally winning him the coveted Magsasay award. An ex-World Bank economist, Shourie became so famous, a household name, until only two years back. He rose to great heights during the Emergency fighting Mrs. Gandhi's tyranny and Sanjay Gandhi's mafia rule. He shook the insipid Indian journalism and became a model to every aspiring journalist. Shourie was the most sought after person till very recently. His writings against Mrs. Gandhi became so intolerable that she prevailed upon the Goenkas to dismiss him. His book, *Hinduism Essence & Consequence*, (Vikas, 1979) is a real masterpiece exposing the hollowness of Hinduism. Critics tore it to pieces and said Shourie being a Punjabi Brahmin should not have exposed the Hindu society to such ridicule. The book is an attempt at placing a mirror before the ugly face of this religion. It was the result of a painstaking research to which we had paid high tributes. It is in this book that Shourie calls Hinduism an intolerant religion preaching hatred and violence against the low castes (pp. 361 & 362).

But the real face of Shourie came to light in his report on the Nellie (Assam) massacre of Muslims. He was silent on the role of Hindu nazis in Assam. S.N.M. Abdi says:

> "He is no longer the unbiased, non-partisan investigator and commentator". (*Illustrated Weekly* Nov. 3, 1985).

That is how the upper caste Assam student leaders fighting against the Bengali Muslims made him their main adviser. His class/caste character got further exposed when he went round the country selling the Hindu nazi stand on Sikhs.

Though he is the general secretary of the People's Union for Civil Liberties, which came out in full support of the Sikhs in the 1984 "Hindu war against the Sikhs" and later published a document on the same, he worked against the interests of the PUCL. He is neither here nor there. If he is genuinely concerned with human rights, he should have sided with the Sikhs as the PUCL and PUDR, another human rights organisation did. Even Tarkunde's Citizens for Democracy brought out a truthful report on the mass murder of Sikhs (*Oppression in Punjab — Report to the Nation*, HMKP Office, 204-Raja Ram Mohan Roy Road, Bombay - 400 004, 1985, pages 130, Rs. 15). But Shourie chose to be with the upper caste Hindus of Punjab. To him his caste became more important than the cause.

This is the secret of his silence for the past two years. What can he write now? How can he say he is a fighter for human rights when the country's topmost human rights organisations have condemned him? How can he say that he fights corruption when he starts praising Indira Gandhi whom he only called as the evil incarnate? He advocated army action against Sikhs as a spokesman of the Hindu nazis and Mrs. Gandhi obliged them. That is how the two became strange bed-fellows. What a mighty fall.

So, which writings of Shourie are to be believed? What he wrote against Mrs. Gandhi during the Emergency calling her a tyrant? Or what he spoke after the "Hindu war against Sikhs" praising her? Which version is true?

Shourie is today a great admirer of the ruling Congress Party and its leader Rajiv Gandhi. Even Rajni Kothari, president of the PUCL, referred to Shourie's right-about-turn at the recent Sikh Forum meeting.

> "Prof.. Kothari also had a dig at the working of the press saying it had become subservient. In a veiled reference, he lamented the switching over of the loyalty of Arun Shourie to Mr. Gandhi". (*Statesman*, Delhi, Nov.3, 1985).

Kothari is not the only person to lament Shourie's fall. We too feel very sad as we had the opportunity of knowing him personally when in the *Indian Express*. Many more have expressed their shock over the fall of this titan.

However, it should be noted that Shourie is not the lone turncoat "intellectual". Barring a couple of names, all these writers, journalists, editors got exposed during the 1984 "Hindu war against Sikhs". Shourie consciously or unconsciously became the victim of a value system which he so mercilessly exposed in his book. He fell into the very well and got drowned after warning others to keep off this danger zone. What happened to all his penchant for investigative journalism? What happened to his fight against fascism? What happened to the fire exhibited in his *Hinduism* book?

What happened to his fight against corruption? What happened to his concern for human rights? What happened to his zeal to blaze new trail in Indian journalism?

Shourie is the standing example of death of a genius. The brahminical value system kills the very genius of India. How can any genius be born in India as long as we see merit in the caste of a person? That is how Shourie's glorious chapter came to abrupt end. Today, he is almost forgotten because his name rarely appears in the press. How can he write? What can he write when he joined the company of Hindu nazis, the fascists, the corrupt, the communal and the wicked?

Arun Shourie is not the only person in India who is suffering this living death. We have taken his name only because he was being hailed as the enfant terrible of Indian journalism, its most famous name. Our entire "intellectual class" with minor exceptions has taken to prostitution. And Arun Shourie is a shining example of that. The value system for which brahminism stands used him and after sucking the juice, it dumped him into the dustbin.

Look at India's English newspapers and language dailies, its gorgeously printed magazines. Barring a couple of them, you find them barren if not vulgar. The same gutter stuff over-flowing with sex, films, sports, money-making tricks, luxury goods and all this with a dash of religion. India has become a sick country packed with sick people. Whole thing is stinking. Just as the people get the govt. they deserve, the people also get the journalists they deserve. That is how India has come to be treated as a pariah in the international arena. Because our "intellectuals" have taken to prostitution. That is how India has become an intellectual wasteland. That is how India has not received a single Nobel Prize since "independence". We hang our head in shame.